# MARIJUANA

BY CAROL HAND

## CONTENT CONSULTANT

### JODI GILMAN, PHD

ASSISTANT PROFESSOR, HARVARD MEDICAL SCHOOL
CENTER FOR ADDICTION MEDICINE, MASSACHUSETTS GENERAL HOSPITAL

Essential Library

An Imprint of Abdo Publishing | abdopublishing.com

ABDOPUBLISHING.COM

Published by Abdo Publishing, a division of ABDO, PO Box 398166, Minneapolis, Minnesota 55439.
Copyright © 2019 by Abdo Consulting Group, Inc. International copyrights reserved in all countries.
No part of this book may be reproduced in any form without written permission from the publisher.
Essential Library™ is a trademark and logo of Abdo Publishing.

Printed in the United States of America, North Mankato, Minnesota
042018
092018

 THIS BOOK CONTAINS
RECYCLED MATERIALS

Cover Photo: Stephen Orsillo/Shutterstock Images
Interior Photos: Brennan Linsley/AP Images, 5; Africa Studio/Shutterstock Images, 8–9; Katarzyna
Bialasiewicz/iStockphoto, 12, 64; Shutterstock Images, 15, 36; iStockphoto, 17, 24, 25 (top right), 25
(top left), 25 (middle left), 32, 35, 38, 45, 48, 50–51, 57, 60–61, 69, 78, 96–97, 98; John Vachon/Library
of Congress/Archive Photos/Getty Images, 20; PA Images/Getty Images, 21; Andris Tkachenko/
iStockphoto, 25 (bottom right); Matt Gibson/iStockphoto, 25 (bottom left); Juan Monino/
iStockphoto, 26–27; Alila Medical Media/Shutterstock Images, 28; Red Line Editorial, 31, 80–81;
Ricardo Arduengo/AP Images, 41; Rick Bowmer/AP Images, 44; D. Keine/iStockphoto, 54; Mary
Altaffer/AP Images, 59; David Maung/Bloomberg/Getty Images, 67; Canna Obscura/Shutterstock
Images, 72–73; Mark Reinstein/Shutterstock Images, 75; Mark Apollo/Pacific Press/LightRocket/
Getty Images, 77; Gregor Bister/iStockphoto, 84; Gilles Mingasson/Getty Images News/Getty
Images, 86–87; Casarsa Guru/iStockphoto, 91; Gillian Flaccus/AP Images, 94

Editor: Valerie Bodden
Series Designer: Laura Polzin

Library of Congress Control Number: 2017961353

Publisher's Cataloging-in-Publication Data
Names: Hand, Carol, author.
Title:  Marijuana / by Carol Hand.
Description: Minneapolis, Minnesota : Abdo Publishing, 2019. | Series: Drugs in real life
     | Includes online resources and index.
Identifiers: ISBN 9781532114175 (lib.bdg.) | ISBN 9781532154003 (ebook)
Subjects: LCSH:  Marijuana--Juvenile literature. | Marijuana abuse--Juvenile literature. |
     Marijuana industry--Juvenile literature. | Drug control--United States--Juvenile
     literature.
Classification: DDC 362.299--dc23

# CONTENTS

# A CONTROVERSIAL DRUG

Zaki Jackson has a rare form of epilepsy. For the first ten years of his life, he suffered hundreds of seizures every day. He could not walk or talk, and sometimes he stopped breathing. According to Dr. Margaret Gedde, one of Zaki's doctors, "His brain could never function well."[1] During the first decade of his life, Zaki's parents tried 17 different drugs, a specialized diet, and alternative therapies such as acupuncture. The medications caused weight gain, cramping, and sleep loss. Some caused him to become confused. But none of them stopped the seizures.

Finally, Dr. Gedde suggested trying a strain of marijuana, or cannabis, known as Charlotte's Web. The drug marijuana comes

from *Cannabis sativa* or *Cannabis indica* plants. While researchers are investigating its value as a medicine, in most areas of the United States it remains an illegal substance. Charlotte's Web has high levels of a chemical called cannabidiol (CBD), which shows promise for treating several illnesses, including epilepsy. It is very low in delta-9-tetrahydrocannabinol (THC). THC is the chemical that causes the euphoric feeling, or high, usually associated with marijuana use. Charlotte's Web is given as a liquid or capsule. It has few or no side effects. The first time Zaki took Charlotte's Web, his seizures stopped for several hours. For the next few months, as his dose was adjusted, the seizures stopped completely. As of October 2017, he had been seizure free for five years.

Not every treatment is as successful as Zaki's, though. Jordan Lyles has a severe form of epilepsy called Dravet syndrome. Her anti-seizure medications left her body limp, so she was unable to speak or eat. After she began treatment with Charlotte's Web, her mother was able to cut Jordan's anti-seizure medications by half. Her seizures have not stopped, but their numbers have decreased significantly.

Sometimes CBD treatment does not work at all. Another young boy with Dravet syndrome had dozens of seizures each day. His family had already tried legal medications, supplements, special diets, and even a treatment used on dogs. The boy's mother, Nicole, had high hopes for Charlotte's Web, but it didn't work. Her son's seizures continued to worsen during CBD use. Even so, Nicole supports the use of cannabis as a treatment. "I've seen firsthand what this has done for other kids, and just because this doesn't work for my son doesn't mean I'm against it," she said. "Knowing what I know now, I would still try it."[2]

## DOCTORS FOR MEDICAL MARIJUANA

Medical marijuana is used to treat seizures and other medical conditions. Dr. David Casarett, author of the book *Stoned: A Doctor's Case for Medical Marijuana*, is convinced of marijuana's medical value. Casarett analyzed published studies, traveled to states where marijuana is legal, and spoke to patients who use the drug. He even tried it for his own

## MOVING FOR MEDICAL TREATMENT

Medical marijuana is legal in Colorado but illegal in many other states. In 2013, the CNN documentary *Weed* featured the story of seven-year-old Charlotte Figi, who was successfully treated with Charlotte's Web. This caused many families to relocate to Colorado to get treatment for their sick children. Some moved from as far away as Canada and Australia. Some separated their families for the move. Paula Lyles moved to Colorado with her daughter Jordan, who suffers from seizures. Her husband and her other daughter stayed in Ohio. Lyles said, "Now I have hope. There was no hope if I had stayed home. I would just be watching her die."[3] Other families agreed that the move to Colorado was worth it, even though it disrupted their lives. "You basically have two choices—you try to do it illegally or you uproot your family, so that's what we did," said Cristi Bundukamara, whose family moved to Colorado from Florida. "This was our only hope."[4]

Many doctors have come to see marijuana as a legitimate treatment for several illnesses.

back pain. Once a skeptic, he changed his mind. "I've come to realize there really are medical benefits to marijuana," he said. "For many of the patients I spoke with, medical marijuana is . . . a treatment that they've come to rely on."[5]

According to Casarett, medical marijuana is particularly helpful in treating neuropathic pain, or pain caused by damaged nerves. The effectiveness of the treatment for any condition varies. It depends partly on the strain of marijuana used, since

different strains have different chemical compositions. It also depends on how the marijuana is taken—whether it is smoked, eaten, or taken in pill form. Casarett advocates serious research on marijuana and its medical effects.

## DOCTORS AGAINST MEDICAL MARIJUANA

Not all doctors support the use of medical marijuana. Doctors who disapprove of using marijuana medically often agree that the plant likely has medicinal value. But they want its medicinal components to undergo strict testing. Before marijuana is adopted for medical use, they want it to meet Food and Drug Administration (FDA) guidelines for safety and effectiveness. They want scientists at the FDA to do more research on marijuana, and they want them to do it faster. They also want the components of marijuana to be dispensed in pill form or in other ways that allow dosages to be carefully measured. These doctors object to the use of raw, smoked marijuana as a medicine. Raw marijuana contains hundreds of unknown, unstudied, and possibly hazardous components. In 2011, raw marijuana failed FDA tests for safety and medical effectiveness.

## THE MANY NAMES OF MARIJUANA

All drugs that contain the chemical THC come from the plant *Cannabis sativa*. Since the early 1900s, these drugs have been lumped together as marijuana. But they also go by a dizzying array of more than 200 nicknames. A few common ones include weed, pot, reefer, dope, ganja, bud, herb, grass, spliff, 420, chronic, Mary Jane, gangster, boom, and skunk. Stronger forms of the drug include sinsemilla, hashish (hash), and hash oil.

Dr. Michael Kirsch is among the doctors who oppose recent state laws legalizing marijuana. Kirsch stated, "I am not against medical marijuana; I am for science."[6] He points out that people who favor the legalization of medical marijuana often rely on polls to make their case. For example, one proponent cited a study showing that 80 percent of Americans think marijuana has medical value.[7] But, Kirsch said, science and evidence, not polls, should determine a drug's safety and effectiveness. So far, the FDA does not think the evidence supports the use of medical marijuana.

## THE MARIJUANA CONTROVERSY

The fact that marijuana is illegal at the federal level has not stopped its use in many states. Medical marijuana has been legal in California since 1996. By 2017, California's medical marijuana industry was worth approximately $2 billion a year.[8] The industry is regulated by the state's 2015 Medical Cannabis Regulation and Safety Act. In the November 2016 election, California voters expanded the state's marijuana use. They approved Proposition 64, the Adult Use of Marijuana Act. This act allowed for the growth and sale of marijuana for recreational use within strict guidelines, beginning on January 1, 2018.

Marijuana is the most widely used illegal drug in the United States. According to the 2015 National Survey on Drug Use and Health, 22.2 million Americans used marijuana in the month before the survey.[9] More males than females used the drug, and use was greatest among adolescents and young adults.

In 2016, 81 percent of 12th-grade students and 35 percent of 8th-grade students reported having easy access to marijuana.[10]

Marijuana is highly controversial in the United States. On one hand, it has been used for thousands of years to treat many

In 2017, 5.9 percent of US twelfth-grade students said they used marijuana daily.

medical conditions. On the other hand, the federal government considers it dangerous and addictive.

Marijuana is considered dangerous for several reasons. First, it causes addiction in some users. In addition, it may negatively affect public safety, such as by impairing drivers and causing accidents. Marijuana may also lead abusers to try more-dangerous drugs, such as heroin, cocaine, or prescription drugs. Smoking marijuana may lead to lung, heart, or mental health conditions. Finally, heavy marijuana use by teenagers is associated with problems in brain development, specifically in the regions controlling learning and memory.

ATrain Education conducts an online course in medical marijuana for health professionals. The organization considers many of the objections to marijuana myths. ATrain points out that marijuana is much less addictive than most drugs and that cannabis itself does not cause people to abuse stronger drugs. Instead, the fact that it must be obtained illegally may lead users to be exposed to other illegal drugs. Some opponents of marijuana say it causes cancer or kills brain cells. But ATrain cites studies showing that marijuana kills cancer cells and may protect brain health. Other opponents suggest that allowing the use of medical marijuana will lead young people to believe the drug is harmless and even good for them. ATrain points out that kids should be taught to respect all medications, including cannabis, and to use them with caution and only as appropriate.

"The idea that this is an evil drug is a very recent construction. . . . For the most part, it was (historically) widely used for medicine and spiritual purposes."[13]

—*Barney Warf, University of Kansas*

In short, the two sides of the controversy hold extreme and sometimes contradictory views. As research into marijuana's potential benefits and dangers continues, the two sides may one day come to an agreement. But debate will likely continue, at least in the near future.

# HISTORY OF MARIJUANA

Most marijuana comes from the plant *Cannabis sativa*. Cannabis probably evolved in the dry plains of central Asia, in the areas now known as Mongolia and southern Siberia. It is among the oldest cultivated plants. At least 12,000 years ago, it flourished in the trash heaps of early hunters and gatherers.

The plant has two major forms. The form used as a drug has psychoactive properties. That is, it acts on the brain and causes changes in the user's perception and mood. It also acts on the body and has been used in many medicines. The other form, known as hemp, is not psychoactive. It has much lower levels of psychoactive chemicals and is used to make products such as

Cannabis grows in many regions but thrives at temperatures between 55 and 86 degrees Fahrenheit (13 to 30°C).

textiles, rope, and oil. The earliest written reference to marijuana as a drug comes from China, in the year 2737 BCE. The reference discusses both psychoactive and medical properties, but the substance's medical uses were considered more important. It was used to treat arthritis, malaria, and absentmindedness.

Marijuana use spread from China to India and then to North Africa. It was used recreationally in both India and North Africa. The Muslim holy book, the Koran, banned the use of alcohol, so marijuana was used instead. Muslims introduced a concentrated form of marijuana known as hashish. Hashish quickly spread throughout Persia (modern-day Iran) and North Africa. Marijuana reached Europe by approximately 800 BCE.

The British introduced hemp to the American colonies in 1611. It quickly became a major crop, grown alongside tobacco. The tobacco was smoked, and the hemp was used as fiber. By the late 1800s, cotton had replaced hemp as a fiber crop

## HEMP THROUGH HISTORY

Hemp is one of the world's oldest cultivated plants. People have woven its fibers since at least 8000 BCE. Cultivation in Great Britain began in approximately 800 CE. In the 1500s, the British navy used hemp fibers in riggings, sails, maps, books, and more. In the 1600s, American farmers were legally required to grow hemp. It was even used as currency. By 1850, American farmers ran 8,400 large hemp plantations.[2] But during the 1930s, a media campaign equated hemp with marijuana, effectively ending the hemp industry.

in the southern United States.

Marijuana, like opium and cocaine, was also used in some medicines in early US history. By the late 1800s, marijuana was sold in pharmacies and doctors' offices as a remedy for stomach pain, vomiting, and other intestinal problems.

In 1943, US farmers harvested 375,000 acres (151,760 ha) of hemp.[3]

## MARIJUANA AND RACISM IN AMERICA

The Spanish brought marijuana to South America in 1545. It moved north into Mexico and made its way into the southwestern United States in the early 1900s. Mexican immigrants brought it north when they fled Mexico during the Mexican Revolution, beginning in 1910. Recreational use of

To process hemp, the plant fibers had to be separated, beaten, scraped, and combed before being woven into useful textiles.

## HOW CANNABIS BECAME MARIJUANA

In the United States, newspapers and medical journals used the word *cannabis* to refer to the drug throughout the 1800s. In the early 1900s, when the first wave of Mexican immigrants began to enter the country, the media began to call the drug *marijuana*. They sometimes spelled it *marihuana* or *mariguana*.

Anti-immigrant groups popularized the word to stoke feelings of fear and hatred toward Mexican immigrants, who used cannabis recreationally. Writers using the word *marijuana* seemed to be describing an entirely different drug than cannabis. They said it caused a "lust for blood" and that smokers were "driven mad," attacking and killing people.[4] At least one article confused marijuana with a poisonous Mexican plant called locoweed. No one knows for sure where the name *marijuana* itself came from. Its origins could be Chinese, Angolan, or Spanish.

marijuana began to catch on in the 1920s, during Prohibition, when the sale of alcohol was banned in the United States. Marijuana was particularly popular among jazz musicians and others in show business. It was not illegal and did not seem to be a social threat as its users did not disturb society. From 1850 through 1941, marijuana was listed in the United States Pharmacopeia—a government-approved list of medications—as a medicine suitable for treating a variety of ailments. People also used the drug to get high.

Prejudice against marijuana and those who smoked it began picking up in the early 1900s. Much of the press on marijuana was outlandish and inaccurate. A 1905 story in the *Los Angeles Times* claimed that "people who smoke marijuana finally lose their mind and never recover it, but their brains dry up and they die, most of times suddenly."[5] The article called the drug "a weed used only by people of the lower class, and sometimes by soldiers."[6] Many stories negatively targeted Mexicans. For example, a 1925 headline in the *New York Times* read, "Mexican, Crazed by Marijuana, Runs Amuck with Butcher Knife."[7] By 1931, 29 states had outlawed cannabis, which the public now feared as the evil weed.

In the 1930s, the federal government began a campaign against marijuana. The US Federal Bureau of Narcotics (now the Bureau of Narcotics and Dangerous Drugs) called marijuana a highly dangerous drug with the potential for addiction. The bureau set out to ban marijuana in all states. The government called marijuana a gateway drug, or a drug that would lead users to abuse stronger drugs. Despite the efforts of the media and the government, marijuana use did not stop. The drug was used by writers and artists in the 1950s and by college students and

## REEFER MADNESS

From the 1930s to the 1950s, films attempted to frighten the public by depicting marijuana as an evil weed that turned people into monsters and drug-addicted fiends. The trailer for the 1936 movie *Reefer Madness* warned of "debauchery, violence, murder, suicide, and the ultimate end of the marijuana addict—hopeless insanity."[8] In the movie, several clean-cut high school students commit rape and other crimes after being lured into smoking marijuana. The movie was so over the top that it became a cult classic, spawning a 2005 musical satire.

The 1938 film *Assassin of Youth* warned of the dangers of marijuana.

hippies in the 1960s. Many people considered marijuana use a symbol of rebellion against authority.

## CONTROLLING MARIJUANA

On October 1, 1937, Congress passed the Marijuana Tax Act. The act put marijuana under the control of the Drug Enforcement Administration (DEA) and made possession of marijuana illegal throughout the country. On October 2, 1937, farmer Samuel Caldwell became the first person arrested under the new law. He was sentenced to four years of hard labor.

In 1970, President Richard Nixon signed the Controlled Substances Act. This act sorted drugs into five schedules, or categories, based on their potential for abuse and their medicinal value. Marijuana was classified as a Schedule I drug.

Drugs in this category are considered to have a high potential for abuse and addiction and no accepted medical use. Other Schedule I drugs include heroin, LSD, and ecstasy. In contrast, both methamphetamines and cocaine are classified as Schedule II drugs. They are considered to have a high potential for abuse, including addiction, but can be prescribed by doctors for specific medical uses. Alcohol and tobacco are not classified at all.

The Controlled Substances Act made it illegal not only to grow, sell, and smoke marijuana but also to grow and sell

Some young people publicly smoked marijuana in the 1960s as a way of rebelling against the government.

industrial hemp. In the early 1970s, President Nixon created the National Commission on Marijuana and Drug Abuse, also known as the Shafer Commission. The commission published a report that recommended changes in federal marijuana laws, although it did not advocate for the legalization of marijuana. The report suggested that law enforcement efforts should focus on marijuana growers and sellers rather than marijuana users.

# STATE LAWS

Many people disagreed with the criminalization of marijuana. Eventually, states began to defy the federal law. California passed the Compassionate Use Act in 1996, making it the first state to legalize the use of marijuana for the treatment of certain severe and chronic illnesses. As of 2017, 29 states, the District of Columbia, Guam, and Puerto Rico had comprehensive medical marijuana programs. Another 17 states allowed the medical use of low-THC products. In 20 states, possession of small amounts of marijuana for recreational use is no longer a felony. Instead, it is considered a misdemeanor, or civil or local infraction, carrying no jail time. In nine states and the District of Columbia, marijuana is legal for recreational use. Several states are now developing methods to license and regulate the cultivation of marijuana and to collect taxes on its sale.

States that have legalized marijuana are protected by the Tenth Amendment of the US Constitution, which reads: "The powers not delegated to the United States by the Constitution, nor prohibited by it to the States, are reserved to the States respectively, or to the people."[9] That is, a state can choose to permit something the federal government prohibits or choose not to help the federal government enforce a law. Federal law enforcement agencies often take no action without help from state law enforcement. However, states are beginning to set up regulatory and licensing schemes for growing marijuana, rather than simply declining to enforce federal laws. This may put them in conflict with federal law. According to marijuana

Marijuana is now legal under certain circumstances in a growing number of states.

attorney Brian Vicente, federal law enforcement officials are unlikely to target consumers simply purchasing marijuana. However, the federal government could shut down businesses selling the drug in violation of federal law, even if their state laws permit marijuana sales.

# TIMELINE OF MARIJUANA

**2737 BCE**
According to legend, a Chinese emperor becomes one of the first people to recommend marijuana tea to treat ailments.

The ancient Egyptians use marijuana to treat inflammation.

**1550 BCE**

The oldest preserved fragment of Chinese hemp cloth dates to this era.

**1122–249 BCE**

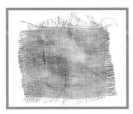

**100–200 CE**
Marijuana is recommended as a medicine and anesthetic in Chinese texts.

**1619**
The Virginia Assembly passes a law requiring all farmers to grow hemp.

The USS *Constitution* is built with hemp sails.

**1797**

Mexican immigrants bring recreational marijuana use to the United States.

**1800s 1920s**
Cannabis is used in over-the-counter medicines in the United States.

**1937**
The Marijuana Tax Act outlaws marijuana.

During World War II, farmers are encouraged to grow hemp for military parachutes and other equipment.

**1940s**

**1970**
The Controlled Substances Act is passed, and marijuana is eventually placed into Schedule I, a category reserved for addictive drugs with no medical use.

**1996**
California becomes the first state to legalize medical marijuana.

**2018**
A total of 29 states allow some use of marijuana.

# CHAPTER THREE

# MARIJUANA AND ITS EFFECTS

Marijuana is sold as a mixture of dried leaves, stems, flowers, and seeds of the cannabis plant. It may appear green, brown, or gray. Marijuana contains more than 400 chemicals.[1] Nearly 120 of these are cannabinoids, a class of molecules unique to the cannabis plant. All cannabinoids are similar, but they vary slightly in size, shape, and chemical structure. Cannabinoids act on structures in the human body known as cannabinoid receptors. Receptors are structures or molecules on a cell's surface that recognize and attach to specific chemicals. As they attach to the receptors, the chemicals activate them, creating

The highest levels of THC are found in the flowering tops, or buds, of female cannabis plants.

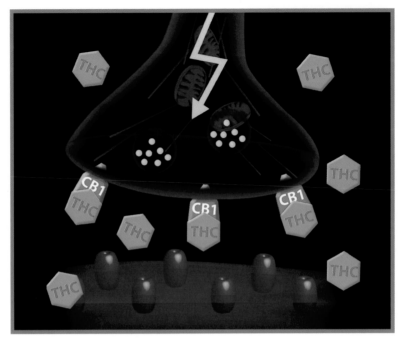

THC fits into CB1 receptors like a key in a lock.

responses in the body. Cannabinoids attach to two known types of cannabinoid receptors. CB1 receptors are found mainly in the brain and central nervous system. CB2 receptors appear mainly in cells of the immune system. Scientists have found some evidence that there may also be a third type of cannabinoid receptor in the blood vessels and lymphatic system.

One of the main components of marijuana is the cannabinoid THC, found largely in the flowers, or buds, of the cannabis plant. THC binds with the brain's CB1 receptors. It causes users to experience intoxication, or a high.

Hashish, or hash, is a more concentrated form of marijuana with a very high THC level. It is a tan, brown, or black resin from the flowers that has been dried and pressed into bars. Both marijuana and hashish have a sweet odor. Other concentrated forms of marijuana include wax, which has a texture similar to lip balm, and shatter, a hard, amber-colored solid. These forms can be dangerous because of their high THC content. In addition, they are often prepared at home using butane, or lighter fluid, which may result in fires or explosions.

Along with THC, marijuana contains CBD, which fits imperfectly into the body's CB1 and CB2 receptors. As a result, it does not activate the receptors. Instead, it blocks certain other chemicals, including THC, from activating them. CBD has important medical effects but does not cause a high. It is used to decrease anxiety and benefit heart health. Research on this compound is just beginning.

## INTERNAL AND EXTERNAL CANNABINOIDS

The human body contains a group of chemicals, called endocannabinoids, that are similar in structure to the cannabinoids in marijuana. Endocannabinoids are recognized by both CB1 and CB2 receptors. THC is structurally similar to the endocannabinoid anandamide, which acts as a neurotransmitter, sending messages between nerve cells in the brain. THC attaches to the same cannabinoid receptors as anandamide. It affects the same brain functions, including pleasure, memory, thinking, coordination, and sensory perception. It also disrupts these functions.

# IMMEDIATE EFFECTS OF MARIJUANA

When someone smokes marijuana, THC moves rapidly from the person's lungs into the bloodstream, which then carries the chemical throughout the body. Once in the brain, THC acts on cannabinoid receptors in areas that control memory, concentration, pleasure, coordination, and sensory and time perception.

Stimulating cannabinoid receptors sets off a chain of chemical reactions, leading to a euphoric feeling, or high. Heart rate increases, balance and coordination decrease, and the user feels dreamy. These sensations usually peak within the first 30 minutes. They wear off within two to three hours. Other physical effects include dizziness, shallow breathing, red eyes, dilated pupils, dry mouth, and increased appetite, often called the munchies. Mental or psychoactive effects include altered senses (such as seeing brighter colors), an altered sense of time, changes in mood,

## CBD AND THE BODY

Researchers have found that CBD influences many receptor systems in the body in addition to cannabinoid receptors. It helps increase levels of the body's own natural cannabinoids, known as endocannabinoids, by preventing them from breaking down. It also influences opioid receptors, which control pain, and dopamine receptors, which help regulate some types of behavior. Finally, CBD activates serotonin receptors, which limit drug-seeking behavior and help decrease anxiety.

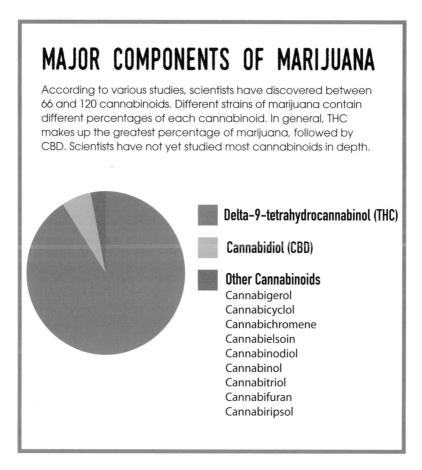

# MAJOR COMPONENTS OF MARIJUANA

According to various studies, scientists have discovered between 66 and 120 cannabinoids. Different strains of marijuana contain different percentages of each cannabinoid. In general, THC makes up the greatest percentage of marijuana, followed by CBD. Scientists have not yet studied most cannabinoids in depth.

**Delta-9-tetrahydrocannabinol (THC)**

**Cannabidiol (CBD)**

**Other Cannabinoids**
Cannabigerol
Cannabicyclol
Cannabichromene
Cannabielsoin
Cannabinodiol
Cannabinol
Cannabitriol
Cannabifuran
Cannabiripsol

impaired memory, impaired movement, and difficulty in thinking and problem solving.

In some marijuana smokers, greatly elevated heart rates and changes in heart rhythms may cause a greater risk for heart attack in the first few hours after smoking. Those at risk of these side effects include older people and people with cardiac risk factors such as high blood pressure or heart arrhythmia. With a very high dose, a person may experience delusions, hallucinations, or even psychosis.

People smoking marijuana don't always think about the way it affects their bodies.

## LONG-TERM EFFECTS OF MARIJUANA

As with any drug, longer periods and higher levels of use increase the chances of health effects. Smoking irritates the lungs, leading long-term marijuana smokers to suffer many of the same health effects as tobacco smokers. They may develop a constant cough, chronic bronchitis, and more frequent colds and pneumonia. In addition, a 2009 study suggested an increased risk of testicular cancer among marijuana users. However, according to Ruben Baler, a health scientist with the National Institute on Drug Abuse (NIDA), early studies showing possible links between lung cancer and marijuana smoking have been overturned by more recent studies.

Babies exposed to marijuana during pregnancy suffer ill effects both before and after birth. They may have lower birth weights. More importantly, marijuana affects the developing brain. When a pregnant woman smokes marijuana, her child has an increased risk for impaired attention, memory, and problem-solving ability. Some THC also enters the mother's breast milk, exposing the baby after birth.

Marijuana can affect brain function and mental health. Long-term use, especially at high levels, can cause the user to be less focused and alert. This compromises the person's ability to carry out complex tasks or meet life goals. Long-term use is also linked to certain types of mental illness in people already predisposed to such conditions. These include temporary hallucinations, temporary paranoia, and worsening symptoms in people with schizophrenia.

Some scientists have also seen links to depression, anxiety, and suicidal thoughts in teenagers, but research results on this are mixed. The immediate effects of marijuana use wear off in a few hours. However, attention, memory, and learning can be affected for several weeks. Thus, a person who uses marijuana almost daily would likely always have impaired mental functioning.

Some long-term users of marijuana may develop a condition known as cannabinoid hyperemesis syndrome, which causes severe nausea, vomiting, and dehydration.

Marijuana use can also lead to addiction. Addiction involves a compulsive need for a substance. Addicted people crave and seek out a substance despite its negative effects on their life. Marijuana is much less addictive than some drugs. Research shows that between 9 and 30 percent of all users become addicted.[2] According to NIDA, people who begin using marijuana before age 18 are four to seven times more likely to become addicted than are people who begin using it as adults.[3] In time, marijuana users may develop a drug tolerance, meaning they require increasingly large doses to get the same effect. If they try to quit, they may suffer withdrawal symptoms. These may include sleeplessness, anxiety, cravings, and decreased appetite. Symptoms begin approximately a day after last use, peak after two to three days, and stop after one to two weeks.

# HOW MARIJUANA IS USED

Cannabis is most often smoked. It can also be delivered orally (through the mouth) or topically (on the skin). Each method provides a different experience because different quantities of active chemicals enter the body. Methods vary in convenience, price, strength, and health effects.

Smoking uses the entire plant, so the smoker receives all of the plant's active compounds. However, amounts are not standardized in each batch. The smoker also inhales many toxic compounds, increasing the risk of lung disease. Cannabis rolled in paper for smoking is known as a joint, while cannabis rolled in cigar coverings made from tobacco leaves is known as a

An average joint holds approximately 0.01 ounces (0.32 g) of marijuana.

Bongs come in a variety of colors, shapes, and sizes.

blunt. Because of the nicotine in their covers, blunts present a greater health risk. Cannabis can also be smoked from pipes or bowls. Water pipes, such as bongs and bubblers, pass the smoke through water before it is inhaled. This cools the smoke but does not filter out toxins.

Some people use vaporization to inhale marijuana. This process is known as vaping. Vaporizers heat the marijuana to temperatures high enough to extract the active ingredients but low enough to prevent the release of most toxic chemicals.

Vaporizers can come in the form of vape pens. These are portable electronic cigarettes that heat up a cartridge of cannabis oil. Vape pens range from pen sized to cigar sized. Other vaporizers are larger and release vapor from dried cannabis into a tube or bag connected to a mouthpiece. Vaping is intended to minimize the health risks of smoking.

Another form of vaporization is dabbing. A dab is a piece of solidified hash oil with an extremely high THC level. It is dropped on a heated construction nail, and the vapor is then trapped in a glass globe and inhaled. The high THC levels make dabbing potentially dangerous.

Consuming marijuana in food—usually brownies, cookies, or cakes—provides a different effect than smoking. When

## SYNTHETIC MARIJUANA

Synthetic cannabinoids are marijuana-like chemicals produced in laboratories. One, known as herbal incense, is sprayed on dried, shredded plant material and then smoked. Liquid incense is vaporized in e-cigarettes. Synthetic marijuana goes by many brand names, including Spice, K2, Black Mamba, Bliss, Bombay Blue, Genie, Moon Rocks, Skunk, Yucatan Fire, and Zohai. These products are sometimes labeled as not for human consumption or as plant food. This allows them to avoid regulation. Although the drugs are often marked as natural, the only natural substance they contain is dried plant material. The drugs themselves are completely manufactured. The DEA has made many of these chemicals illegal, but producers continue to make replacements. Synthetics are often much stronger than natural marijuana. The composition also changes from batch to batch, making their effects unpredictable. In 2015, thousands of people in New York City alone were treated in emergency rooms after using synthetic marijuana.

Marijuana edibles can include everything from cookies and brownies to chocolate bars and lollipops.

people eat marijuana, it takes them 30 to 120 minutes to feel the full effect of the drug. The effect is stronger than when marijuana is smoked. When cannabinoids are digested, they are chemically transformed into stronger substances. Because the effects may last six hours or longer, some people use this method to treat chronic pain. Drinking tea or coffee brewed with marijuana has similar effects.

Marijuana capsules and pills offer more regulated dosages but tend to be highly concentrated. One of the fastest oral delivery methods is the tincture, a concentrated liquid placed on the tongue or sprayed into the mouth. Its effects become apparent within 5 to 15 minutes. In addition to ingesting marijuana, topical creams can be applied directly to the skin. These creams are infused with cannabis high in CBD and are used to treat pain, soreness, and inflammation. They have no psychoactive effects.

Of people treated for marijuana addiction, approximately 41 percent eventually relapse, or begin using the drug again.[4]

# MEDICAL MARIJUANA

The term *medical marijuana* refers to the use of the whole, unprocessed marijuana plant or its extracts to treat illness or other medical symptoms. The FDA has not approved the use of marijuana for medical purposes in the United States. Before approving a drug, the FDA does clinical trials. It tests thousands of people using the drug to analyze its benefits and risks. Benefits must outweigh risks before the FDA gives its approval.

Although the FDA has not given its approval to use of the whole marijuana plant, it has approved the use of two cannabinoids, dronabinol and nabilone, in pill form. Both contain THC. They are prescribed to treat nausea caused by

As of 2016, an estimated 1.2 million Americans legally used medical marijuana.[3]

chemotherapy and to increase appetite in patients with AIDS. Two additional promising drugs have not yet been approved by the FDA. Nabiximols is a mouth spray containing both THC and CBD. It is used to control muscle spasms caused by multiple sclerosis. Epidiolex contains CBD and is used to treat childhood epilepsy.

## WHAT MEDICAL MARIJUANA TREATS

Although large clinical trials have not yet been conducted, experimental research and case studies indicate that medical marijuana may be useful in treating or relieving symptoms of many diseases, including epilepsy and Crohn's disease. Medical marijuana is especially important for pain relief. Chemotherapy patients use it to control both pain and nausea. Harvard University researchers suggest this effect might result from the drug's sedative effect at low doses. Sedation decreases anxiety, which in turn decreases pain and nausea. In high doses, however, marijuana may lead to increased anxiety and paranoia. Marijuana is also useful for treating painful muscle contractions, such as those caused by multiple sclerosis and childhood epileptic seizures. In addition, it has been shown to decrease tremors and pain in people with Parkinson's disease and those with spasms of the diaphragm.

Studies at a San Francisco, California, medical center suggest that marijuana can prevent the spread of cancer by turning off a gene called Id-1. According to several studies in the United States, Israel, and Spain, compounds in marijuana may even kill cancer cells.

Because certain cannabinoids may act on brain systems to lower fear and anxiety, it has been used on veterans suffering from post-traumatic stress

## A SUCCESS STORY

Casey, age 19, developed severe abdominal pains and was losing more than ten pounds (4.5 kg) every week. He was diagnosed with Crohn's disease, an inflammatory bowel disease. His symptoms were so severe that he had to drop out of college. Although medical marijuana is illegal in his state, he began smoking cannabis at a friend's suggestion. The drug helped him begin to gain weight. His doctors quietly supported him, even giving him a prescription for the drug Marinol, an extract of marijuana, in case he was tested for drugs.

In June 2017, patients with various chronic conditions gathered in Utah to advocate for the use of medical marijuana.

## A MEDICAL MARIJUANA REPORT CARD

*Prevention* magazine asked doctors to grade marijuana's ability to treat certain medical conditions. The drug received an A for treating nausea and epilepsy, a B+ for nerve pain relief and Crohn's disease, a B for multiple sclerosis and stopping cancer cell growth, and a B– for reducing tremors in Parkinson's disease. It received C or D grades for treating Alzheimer's, anxiety disorders, PTSD, weight loss, and glaucoma.

disorder (PTSD). However, there have been no clinical trials testing whether marijuana helps with PTSD. A study using a synthetic cannabinoid similar to THC caused a significant decrease in nightmares in PTSD patients. The reasons for this are not yet well understood.

Studies at a British university showed that marijuana may also protect the brain after a stroke. Studies in mice indicate that it may help heal the brain after traumatic injuries, such as concussions. Though research is inconclusive, some doctors advocate allowing football players to use marijuana as a protective agent because many players suffer brain injuries.

## WHAT MEDICAL MARIJUANA CONTAINS

Many people receive the most beneficial medical results when using extracts of the whole marijuana plant. But 5 of

CBD can be purchased as an oil, which can be ingested directly, mixed into food or drinks, or rubbed into the skin.

## CANNABIS VERSUS PRESCRIPTION PAIN RELIEVERS

Opioids are a class of drugs based on compounds found in the opium poppy. These drugs are highly addictive, and overdoses can be fatal. Legal opioids are used as potent painkillers. Prescription opioids include hydrocodone, oxycodone, fentanyl, methadone, and morphine. Heroin is an illegal opioid. Marijuana is much less addictive and dangerous than opioids, and many patients are substituting it for opiate use.

A 2017 study cosponsored by the University of California, Berkeley and HelloMD, a large medical cannabis community, surveyed almost 3,000 people using both opioid and nonopioid pain relievers. Among respondents:

- 97 percent decreased their use of opioids when using cannabis.
- 92 percent preferred cannabis to treat their medical condition.
- 81 percent said using cannabis alone was more effective than using it with opioids.[4]

the nearly 120 cannabinoids in marijuana are often used in medicines. These five are THC, CBD, cannabichromene (CBC), cannabinol (CBN), and cannabigerol (CBG).

THC, best known for its psychoactive properties, may help increase the appetite. CBD is nonpsychoactive and may relieve pain, aid relaxation, and lower anxiety. New strains of marijuana with high CBD concentrations are being developed. These strains contain 15 percent or more CBD and much lower THC concentrations, allowing patients to relieve symptoms without getting high. They are used to treat inflammation, AIDS, epilepsy, chronic pain, and cancer, as well as various psychological conditions, including depression, anxiety, and psychosis.

Like CBD, CBC is not psychoactive. It works well on its own but seems most effective when combined with THC, CBD, or other cannabinoids. It is prescribed for cancer treatment, brain and nerve cell regeneration, depression, and inflammation.

As marijuana ages, some of its THC breaks down to form CBN. This chemical is better than THC and CBD at stimulating appetite. It is also used as an antibiotic, sedative, painkiller, and treatment for asthma, glaucoma, and the progressive muscular disease amyotrophic lateral sclerosis (ALS), also known as Lou Gehrig's disease.

Finally, CBG is another nonpsychoactive cannabinoid and is especially useful as an antibiotic or antimicrobial agent for killing bacteria and other microbes. It is also prescribed for skin ailments, anticancer treatments, and psychological conditions. It is a more potent pain reliever than THC.

## WHAT'S NEXT FOR MEDICAL MARIJUANA?

As of 2017, more than 60 US and international health organizations recommended that medical marijuana be legalized.[5] They have advocated for giving patients immediate access to the drug under a doctor's supervision. Other organizations, including the American Medical Association (AMA), support large clinical

In 2017, the price of medical marijuana ranged from $210 to $603 per one ounce (28 g).[6]

research trials to allow physicians to better determine marijuana's medical potential.

Some people believe that the federal government will eventually legalize marijuana, beginning with medical uses. As more states legalize marijuana use, the trend toward federal

In some cities, people march to promote the legalization of medical marijuana.

legalization will accelerate. People will observe the results in states where the drug is legalized, and if those results are positive, they will be more likely to embrace legalization.

As of 2013, 76 percent of doctors said they would be comfortable prescribing marijuana as a medication if it were legal.[7] However, some doctors would prefer to prescribe it in edible or vaporous form, rather than as a smoking product, due to concerns about lung damage. Some experts currently researching the drug recognize its benefits but are cautious. Dr. Harold Pinnick, professor of chemistry at Purdue University Calumet, said, "There needs to be some way to assess what impact it has under controlled conditions. That is the problem . . . it's not very controlled. We need to do careful studies."[8] Others worry about misuse if marijuana is legalized. Still others see a need to remove the stigma some people would feel about using marijuana. Delivering specific compounds such as CBD rather than whole marijuana might help solve this problem.

## A DOCTOR CHANGES HIS MIND

Dr. Sanjay Gupta, CNN's chief medical correspondent, used to be against medical marijuana. But he has changed his mind. "It doesn't have a high potential for abuse, and there are very legitimate medical applications," Gupta said. "Sometimes marijuana is the only thing that works. We have been terribly and systematically misled for nearly 70 years in the United States, and I apologize for my own role in that."[9]

# CHAPTER FIVE

# MARIJUANA VERSUS TOBACCO AND ALCOHOL

People who advocate for marijuana legalization face opposition from those who consider it a dangerous drug. Those opposed to marijuana legalization emphasize addiction and health risks. Advocates often counter these objections by pointing out the dangers of using tobacco or alcohol. Both are more addictive than marijuana and pose serious health risks. Marijuana advocates

Young people are often exposed to alcohol, tobacco, and marijuana.

ask why these more dangerous drugs are legal while marijuana remains illegal.

While there are decades of rigorous studies on the effects of alcohol and tobacco, there is less data on marijuana. However, as research continues, it is becoming possible to draw some tentative conclusions about the relative dangers of the three drugs.

In 2015, NIDA began a ten-year study following 10,000 young people to assess the effects of alcohol, tobacco, and marijuana on the brain.

## COMPARING DRUG DANGERS

According to the World Health Organization, "On existing patterns of use, cannabis poses a much less serious public health problem than is currently posed by alcohol and tobacco in Western societies."[1] A 2015 study compared the likelihood of death from recreational use of ten drugs: marijuana, alcohol, tobacco, heroin, cocaine, ecstasy, methamphetamine, diazepam, methadone, and amphetamine. The study determined that marijuana was by far the least dangerous of the ten drugs. According to the study's authors, marijuana dangers "may have been overestimated in the past," whereas alcohol risks were "commonly underestimated."[2]

Marijuana, along with heroin and other illegal substances, is classified as a Schedule I drug, placing it among the most dangerous substances. Because alcohol and tobacco are legal, they are not classified. But one in five deaths every year in the United States is due to smoking cigarettes.[3] One in ten deaths is due to alcohol use.[4] There have been no documented overdose deaths due to marijuana use, unless other health factors also contributed to the overdose.

Marijuana advocates also point out its potential in the medical field. A flourishing medical marijuana industry provides relief for thousands of people with a range of medical conditions. There are no corresponding industries for medical alcohol or medical tobacco.

## COMPARING ADDICTION

Some marijuana users become addicted to the drug. But how does marijuana's level of addictiveness compare with those of alcohol and tobacco? US representative Earl Blumenauer of Oregon accidentally caused a review of this question in 2014 when he stated on his website that marijuana was the least addictive of the three. The fact-checking organization PolitiFact analyzed his assertion. After consulting with scientific sources, it rated Blumenauer's statement true.

Dr. J. Wesley Boyd, an addiction expert from Harvard Medical School, agreed that marijuana is less addictive than alcohol or tobacco. He cited a study from NIDA, which found that approximately 9 percent of

In 2016, an estimated 136.7 million Americans over age 12 used alcohol, 51.3 million smoked cigarettes, and 24 million used marijuana.[5]

53

marijuana users, 15 percent of alcohol users, and 32 percent of tobacco users became addicted.[6] Among those who stopped using any of the substances, withdrawal symptoms were worst for alcohol. Alcohol withdrawal causes extremely high heart and pulse rates, seizures, extreme anxiety, and in rare cases, death. Tobacco and marijuana withdrawal are less extreme. Most symptoms are psychological and include sleep disturbances, cravings, and depression.

Other studies have also rated marijuana as less damaging than either alcohol or tobacco in terms of dependence, withdrawal, tolerance, and intoxication. The studies indicate that people become addicted to alcohol and tobacco much more

Once a person becomes addicted to alcohol, it can be difficult to stop drinking without professional help.

quickly than to marijuana and that it is much easier to stop using marijuana than the other two substances. According to studies, the likelihood of becoming addicted to marijuana is much higher for those who begin using the drug in their teens.

But others point out that analyzing the addictive potential of marijuana is difficult because data is limited. In addition, the existing data was collected during a time of prohibition, when use of the drug was illegal. Much of the data is self-reported and thus unreliable. Comparing drugs is also difficult when one is harder to obtain than another. According to NIDA director Nora Volkow, marijuana addiction rates may be low because it is much harder to get a second dose of an illegal drug after

## GIVING USERS A CHOICE

Dr. Carl Hart of Columbia University describes animal drug studies from the 1960s and 1970s in which animals could pull a lever for unlimited access to drugs such as cocaine and methamphetamines. When the cages contained only the drug lever, animals used the drugs until they died. But when given a choice such as a sweet treat or a mate, they often chose the nondrug alternative over the drug. "When given an option, animals do not self-administer drugs until death," Hart said. "The animals will often take the nondrug alternative over the drug."[7] Hart later conducted studies with human drug users. Cocaine users were given a choice of $5 or cocaine. Methamphetamine users were offered a choice between $20 and the drug. The users chose money over drugs at least half the time. According to Hart, who supports the legalization of all drugs, just because drugs are available doesn't mean people will take them, as long as they have other recreational options.

trying it once, making addiction less likely. Volkow fears that if legalization occurs, marijuana will be easier to obtain, leading to an increase in addiction rates.

## THE DANGERS OF SMOKING

Most people consume tobacco and marijuana by smoking. According to the Centers for Disease Control and Prevention (CDC), smoking tobacco is the leading cause of preventable deaths in the United States. It is linked to various cancers including lung cancer, cardiovascular diseases such as heart attacks and strokes, and lung diseases such as chronic obstructive pulmonary disease (COPD).

Like tobacco smoke, marijuana smoke contains many substances, including carcinogens. However, smoke from the two substances is not equally carcinogenic. According to Robert Melamede, deputy director of the National Organization for the Reform of Marijuana Laws (NORML), some of the cannabinoids

### CO-USE OF TOBACCO AND MARIJUANA

In a 2011–2012 survey, more than three-fourths of marijuana users reported also using tobacco.[8] Many co-users also reported using other drugs and being heavy drinkers. Few studies are available on the health effects of co-use, but evidence suggests co-users may find it more difficult to quit marijuana use. They experience more respiratory problems and more severe effects on learning and memory. Co-use in pregnant women increases the likelihood of negative birth outcomes, compared with marijuana use alone.

Research continues into whether marijuana smoke is as harmful as tobacco smoke.

in marijuana smoke are anticarcinogenic, meaning that they may protect against cancer by preventing the activation of certain carcinogens.

Lung specialist Dr. Donald Tashkin participated in the largest known study to investigate the respiratory effects of smoking marijuana. The study concluded that smoking cannabis was not associated with lung cancer, even in heavy users. There was also some suggestion of a protective effect, Tashkin said. Another study showed little evidence of increased lung cancer in marijuana users, and a third study showed a significant decrease in head and neck cancers among marijuana smokers. Marijuana also appears not to increase COPD risk.

Ruben Baler of NIDA agrees that no association has been found between lung cancer and marijuana smoking. He thinks this may be due either to beneficial compounds in marijuana smoke or to the fact that marijuana users smoke less often than tobacco smokers. Typical tobacco users smoke 10 to 20 cigarettes per day; marijuana smokers may smoke only two or three times per month.[9] Baler cautions that more study is needed to understand the reasons behind the results.

According to some studies, lung airflow rate actually increases with marijuana smoking. A 20-year study of more than 5,000 young adults showed that although cigarette smokers lost lung function, low to moderate marijuana smokers increased their lung capacity.[10] The reason is unknown, but researchers suggest it might result from marijuana smokers breathing more deeply or smoking less frequently than tobacco smokers. However, among the heaviest marijuana smokers, lung capacity decreased.

Others disagree that marijuana is nearly harmless when smoked. The American Lung Association (ALA) notes that marijuana smoke contains many of the same toxins as tobacco smoke. Also, marijuana smokers take longer, deeper inhalations at higher combustion temperatures than cigarette smokers. According to the Foundation for a Drug-Free World, "The typical user inhales more smoke and holds it longer than he would with a cigarette. . . . Smoking one joint gives as much exposure to cancer-producing chemicals as smoking four to five cigarettes."[11] Marijuana joints release five times more carbon monoxide and three times more tar than cigarettes. One-third more tar from joints remains in the respiratory tract, where it damages the lungs and can lead to lung and throat cancer.[12] Marijuana smoke also contains more ammonia and hydrogen cyanide than cigarette smoke.

Marijuana smoke can also have a negative impact on the immune system, especially in users with already weakened immune systems. Secondhand marijuana smoke is likely to be dangerous, too, especially to children. Despite these dangers, the ALA advocates continued research, especially on lung health. It favors medical marijuana use, in consultation with a doctor, if the patient uses a delivery method other than smoking.

A lifetime of cigarette smoking can turn healthy lungs, *left*, into a diseased mass, *right*.

# CHAPTER SIX

# MARIJUANA IN SOCIETY

Drugs can impact individuals' school, work, and social lives. This can translate into effects on society at large. Experts study how drug use relates to such things as crime rates, public health, and economics.

## WHO USES MARIJUANA?

According to a CDC study, US marijuana use is rising. Between 2002 and 2014, marijuana use increased among adults age 18 or older but not among teens ages 12 to 17. In 2014, approximately 2.5 million people ages 12 and older used marijuana for the first time. This means approximately

Teens may find themselves in situations where marijuana is readily available.

7,000 people become new marijuana users every day.[1] However, dependence and abuse of marijuana decreased, except among adults ages 26 and older. The study's authors suggested that increased use among adults might be due to greater ease of obtaining the drug or fewer penalties for its use.

Marijuana use by adolescents in grades 8, 10, and 12 peaked in the mid-1990s, declined gradually through the mid-2000s, and then leveled off. It declined slightly again between 2010 and 2015. Marijuana use increases as teens age. In 2016, 9.4 percent of eighth graders, 23.9 percent of tenth graders, and 35.6 percent of twelfth graders had used marijuana in the past year. During the month before the survey, 5.4 percent of eighth graders, 14 percent of tenth graders, and 22.5 percent of twelfth graders had used the drug. Six percent of twelfth graders said they used it daily or almost daily.[2]

The Drug Abuse Warning Network (DAWN) monitors the health impact of drugs. In 2011, the organization documented almost 456,000 emergency room visits in which marijuana was mentioned. Two-thirds of the patients were male; 13 percent were between ages 12 and 17. The numbers for 2011 represented a 21 percent increase from the number of marijuana-related emergency room visits in 2009.[3] DAWN

Between 1998 and 2008, world consumption of opiates increased by 35 percent, cocaine use by 27 percent, and marijuana use by 9 percent.[4]

suggested that the increase might have been due to increased use of marijuana or increased potency in the marijuana consumed. It noted that not all emergencies were necessarily caused by marijuana use; rather, marijuana use was simply mentioned in the patients' medical records.

Worldwide, cannabis use is increasing, according to United Nations data for the years 2009 through 2013. Trends in the Americas and Europe showed declines in cocaine use and increases in cannabis and nonmedical use of prescription opioids during this time. The increased number of people being treated for cannabis use disorders around the world suggests that cannabis may be becoming more harmful. This is most likely due to improved cultivation techniques and genetic strains that maximize THC percentages.

## CHANGING MARIJUANA POTENCY

The potency of marijuana is measured by its concentration of THC, the plant's psychoactive ingredient. Marijuana potency is increasing. Researchers analyzed 38,600 samples of illegal marijuana confiscated by the DEA over a period of 20 years. The average THC concentration in 1995 was 4 percent; the average in 2014 was 12 percent. Another study, done in Colorado, showed the same trend. In 1985, Colorado samples contained less than 10 percent THC. In 2015, levels were up to 30 percent. As THC has increased, the medically useful component, CBD, has declined from 0.28 percent in 2001 to less than 0.15 percent in 2014.[5]

# EFFECTS ON SCHOOL, WORK, AND HEALTH

Every drug has a profile of side effects, or a list of unintended negative effects that accompany its use. If a drug is overused or used chronically, its side effects can take a serious toll on the user's physical and mental health.

Because of its effects on the memory and judgment regions of the brain, heavy marijuana use can harm learning and attention skills. Teenage users show lower achievement and more delinquency than nonusers, as well as more aggressive behavior and rebelliousness. They also have more difficulty with parents and associate more with other drug users.

A review of 48 studies indicated that marijuana use was associated with lower graduation rates in students. Three studies in Australia and New Zealand showed that teen users were less likely to finish high school or obtain a degree. They were also more likely to become addicted, use other drugs, and attempt suicide. A few studies link marijuana use to decreased income, unemployment, criminal behavior, and lower life satisfaction. But these associations do not prove marijuana causes these problems. Other factors may be involved. US studies contradict some results of the Australian review. For example, according to a 2014 study in the *American Journal of Public Health*, men between ages 20 and 39 who used marijuana showed a 10.8 percent reduction in suicide rates.[6]

Adolescents, especially if they are inexperienced marijuana users or take heavy doses, are vulnerable to mental health issues resulting from marijuana use. These include anxiety and panic attacks, depression, and psychotic illnesses such as schizophrenia. However, psychosis associated with marijuana use is likely to occur only in people with a genetic history of the disease or in those who have suffered abuse.

For adults, workplace impacts of marijuana depend on the type of work being performed. Because of their need for concentration and good memory, people who perform highly technical tasks are more likely to be affected than those who do manual labor. Long-term or heavy use, especially if it started in adolescence, can cause continuing problems with decision-making and planning.

## DRUGGED DRIVING

Because marijuana affects the cerebellum, the part of the brain that controls balance and coordination, its use can affect driving. Users have slower reaction times, impaired judgment, and difficulty responding to sounds and signals. A study showed that marijuana users are twice as likely as sober persons to be involved in traffic collisions. However, people with blood alcohol concentrations of 0.08 or higher are 4 to 27 times more likely than sober people to experience a collision.[7] According to one study, THC impairs driving ability, but drivers tend to overcompensate by driving more slowly. Alcohol users, in contrast, drive faster and take more risks.

Although Mexican officials have tried to stop the illegal marijuana trade by seizing and burning supplies of the drug, some marijuana still makes it across the United States–Mexico border.

## MARIJUANA AND CRIME

From a law enforcement perspective, the illegal buying and selling of marijuana increases crime and violence, especially at the United States–Mexico border. Some marijuana sold in the United States is smuggled into the country from Canada or Mexico. Other imported illegal marijuana comes from Colombia, Jamaica, Thailand, Kazakhstan, Nigeria, and South Africa. Within the United States, marijuana is often grown illegally in national forests or in people's homes.

According to a 2015 article in *US News & World Report*, "Drug crime is the leading path into the federal prison system, and Americans put more people in federal prison for crimes related to marijuana than any other drug."[8] In 2015, there were ten times as many people in US prisons for drug-related crimes as in 1980. Approximately one-half had committed nonviolent crimes, most involving marijuana possession and use.[9]

Marijuana accounted for approximately 43 percent of all drug arrests in 2015. A total of 575,000 people—nearly one person a minute—were arrested on marijuana charges. The United States spends nearly $3.6 billion a year enforcing marijuana laws.[10]

The rise in prisoners has resulted in massively overcrowded prisons. According to Bureau of Prisons (BOP) director Charles Samuels Jr., the BOP accommodates excess prisoners by putting two or three bunks in a single cell and converting television rooms and open areas into sleeping quarters. Such conditions can endanger the lives of both inmates and corrections officers.

In addition, many people convicted of marijuana possession receive long sentences. A New Orleans, Louisiana, truck driver was

## RACIAL DISPARITIES

Data from 2001 through 2010 from the American Civil Liberties Union showed who was arrested for marijuana possession. Although African Americans and whites used marijuana at approximately equal rates, African Americans were almost four times more likely to be arrested for possession.[11] From 2012 to 2016, African Americans and Hispanics made up less than 50 percent of the population of Buffalo, New York, but represented 86 percent of arrests for marijuana violations. In Pennsylvania, black adults were 8.2 times more likely than whites to be arrested for possession.[12]

Marijuana possession is grounds for heavy fines or imprisonment in some states.

sentenced to more than 13 years for having a small amount of marijuana in his pocket. A Missouri man, arrested in 1993, was sentenced to life without parole for possession of a 5-pound (2.3 kg) brick of marijuana, which he claimed to be unknowingly involved in selling. Both sentences were particularly harsh because each man had two previous nonviolent offenses. Even after a nonviolent drug offender is released from prison, the arrest stays on his or her record for years. This limits the individual's ability to obtain a job, loan, housing, and other benefits.

## THE MARIJUANA GATEWAY?

Some people believe that marijuana is a gateway drug. That is, people who use the drug are more likely to later use other drugs as well. Robert L. DuPont, former director of NIDA, described marijuana in this way, saying it leads to the use of harder drugs, particularly heroin. He cited the fact that most heroin users begin in their teens, and they also use alcohol and marijuana. In 2017, Homeland Security secretary John Kelly echoed DuPont's belief, calling marijuana "a dangerous gateway drug."[13] According to at least one study, marijuana primes the brain to respond to other drugs.

However, Miriam Boeri, an associate professor of sociology at Bentley University, strongly contradicts the gateway drug theory. She points out that co-use of marijuana and harder drugs proves only that use of one drug may correlate with use of other drugs, not that the use of marijuana causes the use of other drugs. According to the Institute of Medicine of the National Academy of Sciences:

> *Because it is the most widely used illicit drug, marijuana is predictably the first illicit drug most people encounter. Not surprisingly, most users of other illicit drugs have used marijuana first. In fact, most drug users begin with alcohol and nicotine before marijuana—usually before they are of legal age. In the sense that marijuana use typically precedes rather than follows initiation of other illicit drug use, it is indeed a "gateway" drug. But because underage smoking and alcohol use typically precede marijuana use, marijuana is not the most common, and is rarely the first, "gateway"*

*to illicit drug use. There is no conclusive evidence that the drug effects of marijuana are causally linked to the subsequent abuse of other illicit drugs.*[14]

# MARIJUANA AND THE ENVIRONMENT

Illegal marijuana cultivation is causing increasingly serious environmental damage. Cultivation frequently occurs on public lands, such as national forests. Growers cut down native vegetation, allowing non-native plants to invade. They dam streams for irrigation, damage downstream habitats, and create wildfire hazards. They discard garbage and highly toxic insecticides used in growing marijuana. They

## A TOWN'S NEGATIVE EXPERIENCE WITH MARIJUANA

After Colorado legalized recreational marijuana in 2012, the small town of De Beque grew commercial cannabis to increase its income. The town handed out many licenses to growers but overlooked the problem of pesticide use. Because marijuana is illegal under federal law, no pesticides are approved for use on marijuana plants. Growers made their own pesticide mixtures, some so toxic that several facilities had to be quarantined in 2015. Peach farmers in a neighboring town worried about the spread of molds and other pests from cannabis fields to their orchards. Further, the town has experienced marijuana-intoxicated driving, illegal movement of marijuana into nearby states, increased marijuana use among teens, more emergency room visits, and even an exploding homeless population as consequences of marijuana legalization.

The bright lights, powerful fans, and intricate watering systems of indoor marijuana-growing facilities consume large amounts of water and electricity.

pollute watersheds, groundwater, and eventually residential water supplies.

Even when grown legally, marijuana can impact the environment. A single cannabis plant requires 6 gallons (23 L) of water a day. Marijuana grown in indoor greenhouses

uses massive amounts of electricity to run the bright lights, ventilators, dehumidifiers, and climate-control systems required. In 2012, 3 percent of all electricity use in California went to the cultivation of indoor marijuana.[15] All that power consumption leads to increases in the release of carbon emissions.

# TO LEGALIZE OR NOT TO LEGALIZE

In 2017, a war of sorts occurred over the future of marijuana in the United States. On one side were opponents of legalization, including Attorney General Jeff Sessions, who described marijuana as "only slightly less awful" than heroin.[1] Sessions considered marijuana a dangerous drug and was determined to crack down, especially on recreational marijuana use. He wanted to return to the restrictive drug policies of the 1980s and 1990s, which stressed criminalizing drug use to prevent abuse. Sessions said, "Educating people and telling them the terrible truth about drugs and addiction will result in better choices."[2] He threatened to seize the money and property of those suspected

Attorney General Jeff Sessions has been among the most outspoken opponents of marijuana legalization.

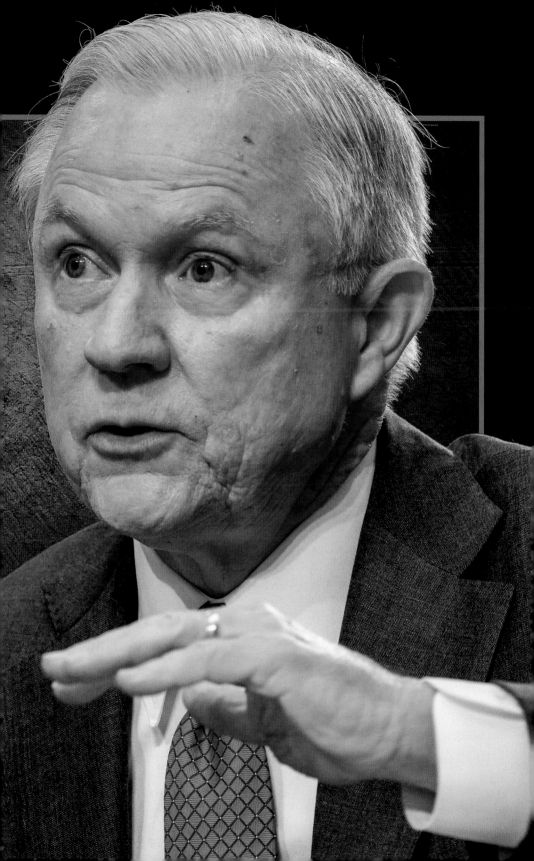

of drug trafficking. Some in the marijuana industry feared he could also use these threats against cannabis businesses. Shortly after taking office, Sessions set up a task force to review drug enforcement. He rolled back lighter sentencing guidelines created by the administration of President Barack Obama, and he directed prosecutors to charge offenders with the most serious possible crimes. He recommended rolling back amendments that prevent the federal government from interfering with marijuana enforcement at the state level.

On the other side of the argument was the majority of the American population. According to an April 2017 CBS News poll, 61 percent of Americans favored legalizing marijuana, 71 percent thought the federal government should not interfere with states that have legalized it, and 88 percent thought medical marijuana should be legal.[3] In August 2017, Senator Cory Booker of New Jersey introduced a bill that would eliminate marijuana from the federal

## CONFLICT OF INTEREST

The DEA has the power to revise drug classifications and classify new drugs. It acts on the recommendations of the Department of Health and Human Services, which conducts scientific and medical studies. Although the DEA maintains that it schedules drugs based purely on science, some feel the DEA's role represents a conflict of interest. According to journalist Harrison Jacobs, "The law-enforcement agency whose budget depends explicitly on the magnitude of the threat from illegal drugs is in charge of determining the dangerousness of those drugs, rather than a scientific or medical body."[4]

list of Schedule I drugs. This would decriminalize marijuana throughout the country. Booker's bill also encouraged states to legalize marijuana. The bill had no chance of passing Congress, but its introduction showed how far the push toward legalization had come since the first states legalized recreational marijuana in 2012.

Nearly 70 percent of millennials (born between 1981 and 1997) support legalizing marijuana, compared with only 29 percent of those born between 1928 and 1945.[5]

## PROS OF LEGALIZATION

The controversy over legalizing marijuana will likely continue for some time. This is partly because people simply have opposing

Cannabis supporters use creative techniques to share their message.

opinions about drug use of any kind. It also relates to the uncertain nature of the evidence. Research on marijuana effects is limited and sometimes contradictory. Data on the drug's social impact is limited, and the data available is sometimes tainted by the biases of the interpreters.

From a health viewpoint, marijuana is less dangerous than alcohol or tobacco, both of which are legal. In addition, marijuana exhibits numerous health benefits and successfully treats many

In places where marijuana is legal, people may be able to buy seeds to grow limited quantities of their own cannabis plants.

diseases. It can provide less-addictive alternatives to commonly used pain management drugs for many patients.

From a law enforcement perspective, legalizing marijuana nationwide could lead to the dismantling of parts of the black market. With legal, regulated dispensaries, or marijuana stores, underground sales would no longer be needed. Because legal marijuana is regulated, customers receive a safer, higher-quality product than when purchasing illegal, unregulated street drugs.

Removal of marijuana as an illegal product would also eliminate one source of drug violence. Decriminalization would eliminate the need to arrest and prosecute those using marijuana. Resources once used for enforcement of marijuana laws could be directed toward more-serious crimes. In addition, people using the drug would not face the current harsh penalties that often lead to job loss and other negative outcomes.

"Penalties against possession of a drug should not be more damaging to an individual than the use of the drug itself; and where they are, they should be changed."[6]

—President Jimmy Carter, Drug Abuse Message to Congress, August 2, 1977

Financially, the legalization of marijuana could lead to economic benefits. Marijuana is a major agricultural product. Legalization would result in tax revenues that would benefit the US economy.

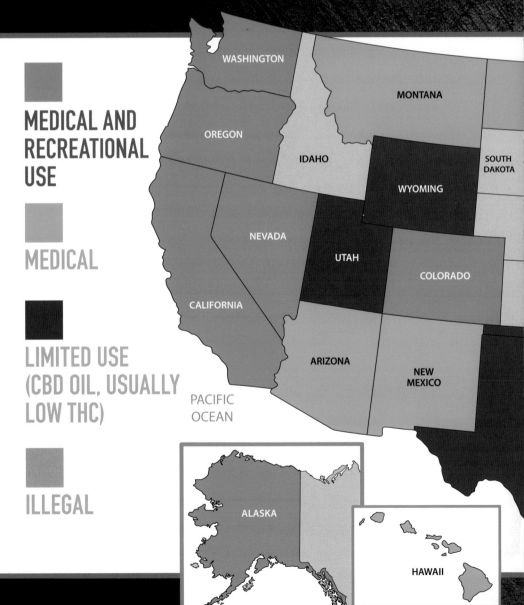

# STATUS OF STATE CANNABIS LAWS

**MEDICAL AND RECREATIONAL USE**

**MEDICAL**

**LIMITED USE (CBD OIL, USUALLY LOW THC)**

**ILLEGAL**

WASHINGTON

MONTANA

OREGON

IDAHO

SOUTH DAKOTA

WYOMING

NEVADA

UTAH

COLORADO

CALIFORNIA

ARIZONA

NEW MEXICO

PACIFIC OCEAN

ALASKA

HAWAII

As of January 2018, 29 states and the District of Columbia had legalized marijuana either for medical use or for medical and recreational use. A number of states also allowed for limited medical use of low-THC marijuana in certain circumstances. In 6 states, marijuana use remained completely illegal.

## ORGANIZATIONS PRO AND CON

Probably the best-known US organization favoring marijuana legalization is NORML, founded in 1970. NORML's goal is to change public opinion, leading to the legalization of marijuana for responsible adult use. The Marijuana Policy Project (MPP), founded in 1995, seeks to change federal law to allow states to determine their own marijuana policies.

Organizations opposed to marijuana legalization include Citizens Against Legalizing Marijuana (CALM). This all-volunteer group works to defeat any state law that undermines the federal Controlled Substances Act. Smart Approaches to Marijuana (SAM) advocates a science-based approach to marijuana education and awareness. It is concerned that the marijuana industry is poised to become another version of the tobacco industry, with a goal of profiting from addiction.

# CONS OF LEGALIZATION

On the con side of the argument, many people consider drug use immoral. In addition, marijuana poses health dangers, including lung damage, addiction, and mental health problems. Bystanders can suffer from the consequences of secondhand smoke. Some people also argue that marijuana serves as a gateway drug, leading to the use of harder drugs.

In terms of law enforcement, some opponents believe that people who buy and sell marijuana are more likely to be involved in other crimes and that jailing them will decrease crime rates. Some law enforcement officials do not want to be associated with any support of drug use. Opponents also fear that the altered perceptions stemming from marijuana use will lead more people to drive while impaired. In addition, decreased inhibitions from marijuana use could lead users to commit violent crimes.

# CURRENT MARIJUANA LAWS

States continue to liberalize marijuana laws. Medical marijuana legalization (MML) began in 1996, long before states began approving recreational use. As of 2018, 29 states plus the District of Columbia, Guam, and Puerto Rico had adopted extensive medical marijuana programs. Another 17 states had legalized the use of low-THC marijuana for medical purposes. Legalization of marijuana for recreational use began in 2012, and 9 states and the District of Columbia had legalized it by January 2018.

As of 2017, Colorado had more than 500 licensed marijuana stores and more than 700 licensed marijuana cultivators.[8]

In 2017, 41 percent of the US population had access to medical marijuana. Another 35.4 percent was allowed medical use of low-THC, high-CBD marijuana, while 21.3 percent had access to marijuana for recreational use. Only 2.3 percent were completely prohibited from using marijuana.[7]

Though many people acknowledge the potentially damaging effects of marijuana, they feel its level of harm can best be handled by providing strong regulation as is done with alcohol and tobacco. States are just beginning to figure out how to regulate marijuana use. They are working on ways to collect taxes

Like alcohol use, marijuana use carries the risk of accidents due to impaired driving.

and to regulate and license marijuana cultivation and sales. They are trying to address safety concerns. Colorado and Washington, for example, have set a maximum allowance of five nanograms of THC per milliliter of blood for marijuana content in blood. Above this level, an individual is considered too impaired to drive. States are also working on ways to ensure marijuana access for adults over age 21 while preventing access to children. Methods include requiring identification before sale, as is done with tobacco and alcohol; child-resistant packaging; and prohibiting people from using it in public. States are also developing research and public education programs.

State and federal marijuana regulations still clash. In October 2009, the Obama administration relaxed federal interference with state marijuana laws, encouraging federal prosecutors not to prosecute people distributing marijuana in states with MML. In August 2013, the Department of Justice (DOJ) announced it would not challenge state legalization laws as long as states developed "strong, state-based enforcement efforts."[9] Most states with MML have some form of patient registry to indicate those legally using medical marijuana and protect them from prosecution by federal authorities.

In 2017, Attorney General Jeff Sessions reinstated earlier strong enforcement policies. However, Sessions faced resistance from Congress. In May 2017, Congress passed a temporary budget that included an amendment blocking the DOJ from prosecuting marijuana growers, sellers, and users in states with MML. Also in May, a bipartisan group of lawmakers introduced the Therapeutic Hemp Medical Access Act, designed to ensure

## ABUSING MEDICAL MARIJUANA?

Some people believe that medical marijuana laws can be abused by people without a medical need for the drug. According to Kevin Sabet of the Center for Substance Abuse Solutions at the University of Pennsylvania, "A recent study found that the average 'patient' (using medical marijuana) was a 32-year-old white male with a history of drug and alcohol abuse and no history of a life-threatening disease."[10]

The sale of marijuana in legitimate stores may eliminate crimes related to purchasing the drug illegally.

that people with severe epilepsy could obtain high-CBD strains of marijuana. If passed, the law would represent an exemption to the Controlled Substances Act.

## HOW LEGALIZING MARIJUANA CHANGES SOCIETY

People are just beginning to study social changes in states that have legalized marijuana. Claims about its societal effects vary according to political leanings. Conservative critics of legalization

expect widespread marijuana availability to increase crime, damage public health, and increase traffic accidents. Liberal supporters of legalization make the opposite claims. They also expect an improved economy due to increased tax revenues and decreased criminal justice costs because there are fewer criminal charges for drug possession.

Studies by various government organizations and universities show that those states where marijuana is legal have not experienced increased marijuana use or changed attitudes toward the drug. The *Journal of Public Health* reported no obvious changes in health-care systems in areas where marijuana has been decriminalized but "substantial savings in the criminal justice system."[11]

One immediate effect of marijuana legalization or decriminalization may be a drop in crime rates because marijuana users are no longer being jailed. Several studies indicate that crime has been reduced in states where medical marijuana legalization has occurred. Harvard researcher David Trilling cautioned that although this demonstrates a relationship between marijuana legalization and lower crime rates, it does not prove that one causes the other.

A Colby College study demonstrated a 4 to 12 percent drop in property crimes, including theft and burglaries, after MML. Crime overall has fallen 5 percent more in states with MML than in states without it.[12] Robert G. Morris and colleagues, of the University of Texas, found that crime rates fell in every state

## EFFECTS OF LEGALIZATION IN CALIFORNIA

Beginning January 1, 2011, the state of California fully decriminalized marijuana. Opponents predicted harmful effects on teenagers, but the opposite happened, according to a 2014 report from the Center on Juvenile and Criminal Justice. Crime rates, drug overdoses, and cases of driving under the influence all improved after the reform. In addition, school dropout rates declined by 22 percent.[13] However, experts cautioned that these results may not have been caused by marijuana's legalization and that the study covered only a few years.

that introduced MML. They attributed this to more people turning to marijuana in place of alcohol. They concluded, "Given the relationship between alcohol and violent crime, it may turn out that substituting marijuana for alcohol leads to minor reductions in violent crimes."[14] Although recreational marijuana has been legal in fewer states and for a shorter time than medical marijuana, early studies suggest that recreational legalization, too, lowers crime rates. For example, when Washington legalized marijuana, the murder rate fell by 13 percent, overall violent crime by 10 percent, and burglaries by 6 percent.[15]

In 2016, the Cato Institute, a conservative think tank, published a preliminary review of marijuana use in four states where recreational marijuana was legalized: Colorado, Washington, Alaska, and Oregon. They found only modest changes in marijuana use and effects after legalization. There was no evidence for the strong claims made by either advocates or critics of legalization. Both marijuana use and prices continued the trends they had demonstrated before legalization—a slight increase in use coupled with a slight decrease in price. The institute concluded: "The absence of significant adverse consequences is especially striking given the sometimes dire predictions made by legalization opponents."[16] However, the organization stressed that legalization in these states was still relatively new and stronger conclusions would be possible only after more time had passed.

# CHAPTER EIGHT

# MARIJUANA TODAY AND TOMORROW

States continue to loosen their restrictions on the growth, sale, and use of marijuana, but the federal government has retained the drug's Schedule I standing. As of 2017, about three-fourths of US citizens had access to medical marijuana, although for more than one-third, that access was limited to a few specific strains or extracts.[1]

## THE FEDERAL APPROACH TO MARIJUANA

Throughout the years, various medical organizations—including the AMA—have recommended rescheduling marijuana as a medical drug. A 2014 survey of 1,500 doctors showed that

As more states legalize marijuana, research into the drug's effects will likely increase.

56 percent favored legalizing medical marijuana nationally. Among oncologists, or cancer physicians, the figure was 82 percent.[2] But in August 2016, the DEA reviewed its placement of marijuana and chose to keep it as a Schedule I drug. DEA chief Chuck Rosenberg stated that the decision was based on science, particularly on the recommendation of the FDA. "This decision isn't based on danger," Rosenberg said. "This decision is based on whether marijuana, as determined by the FDA, is a safe and effective medicine, and it's not."[3]

New York University professor Mark Kleiman thinks the solution is to open up marijuana research to the scientific community. There is a lack of evidence on marijuana's medical benefits, partly because the DEA restricts the amount of marijuana used in research. Both the DEA and the FDA say they are open to research on medical marijuana. Since December 2015, they have made it easier to conduct research on the treatment of epilepsy with CBD. They also plan to make it

## DECRIMINALIZING TO STOP ADDICTION

While the United States has tried to solve its drug problem with stricter penalties, other countries have tried different methods. In the 1990s, Portugal had a serious drug addiction problem. Prison was not helping. So the country decided to legalize drugs. The money that had previously gone toward prosecuting and jailing drug offenders was instead invested in drug treatment programs and public health. Within a decade, drug addiction dropped by one-half.[4]

easier to conduct legitimate research on marijuana by allowing more individuals and universities to grow the plant for research purposes. As of 2018, only one site, the University of Mississippi, was allowed to do this.

# LEGALIZATION— WHEN AND HOW?

Marijuana supporters are optimistic about the future of medical marijuana. As the number of states legalizing marijuana for both medical and recreational uses has increased, a booming industry has resulted. The marijuana industry now includes everything from marijuana cultivation to the production and sale of joints and vaporizers and the development of food products containing the drug. Investors are also pouring money into research for new technology for growing and testing marijuana. A whole market has also opened

Approximately 22 million pounds (10 million kg) of marijuana are grown in the United States every year. Eighty percent is grown in California, Tennessee, Kentucky, Hawaii, and Washington.[5]

## GOVERNMENT POT SHOP

The city of North Bonneville, Washington, needed money. So after Washington legalized marijuana in 2012, the city decided to establish its own marijuana shop. The shop, named Cannabis Corner, opened in 2015. It sells a variety of cannabis products and accessories. Profits from the shop are used to fund public health initiatives in the city. According to North Bonneville mayor Don Stevens, "The overall guideline is to use the money for anything that has a positive impact on public health and safety in our community."[6]

around cannabis-themed businesses, such as cannabis-friendly bed-and-breakfasts, painting classes, and even bike tours.

Even in states with legalized marijuana, however, the federal prohibition causes problems for the industry. Banks cannot legally take money from marijuana dispensaries; thus, marijuana businesses must complete all transactions in cash. This is inconvenient and often dangerous, as it increases the likelihood of robberies. Governor John Hickenlooper of Colorado, a state where marijuana is legal, has asked the US Congress to pass legislation that prevents federal regulators from penalizing banks that serve the marijuana industry. Congress itself is beginning to act as well. In February 2017, a bipartisan group including Representative Jared Polis of Colorado formed the Congressional Cannabis Caucus. The caucus plans to develop and pass federal legislation to help states with legalized marijuana. According to Polis, federal marijuana prohibition has failed. He believes

## WILDFIRES BURN CALIFORNIA CROP

In October 2017, up to 200,000 acres (81,000 ha) in northern California burned in rampant wildfires. At least 42 people were killed, and 34 marijuana farms, along with their crops and buildings, were seriously damaged by fire, smoke, and ash.[7] Because the federal government considers marijuana farming and sales illegal, marijuana growth is not a fully legitimate business. Growers have difficulty getting mortgages and loans. Most have no insurance to replace lost crops and buildings. Growers cannot receive federal disaster relief.

Some people believe that the war against marijuana use has caused more problems than the drug itself.

it is time for Congress to help, rather than hinder, states' legalization attempts.

Support for marijuana legalization is highest among young people and their parents, many of whom have tried the drug.

According to Greenberg Quinlan Rosner Research, the rise in the
number of people who favor legalization is most likely due to
two factors. First is the belief of many that the personal, social,
and economic costs of current drug laws have been greater

As marijuana use becomes more widely legalized, stores like this may spring up in more places.

than their benefits. According to Dr. Evan Wood, scientific chair of the International Centre for Science in Drug Policy, there is a "growing body of evidence that the war on drugs has failed."[8]

The marijuana industry in the United States earned more than $6.7 billion in 2016 and was growing at a rate of 25 to 30 percent a year.[9]

Wood recommends treating drug use as a public health issue, rather than a criminal justice issue. Second is the belief that legalizing and regulating marijuana could raise millions of dollars in tax revenues that could be used for social services, including improving schools.

In his book *Marijuana: A Short History*, John Hudak of the Brookings Institution assumes that marijuana legalization is inevitable. He sees the current prohibition as simply a hiccup in the process of finding the best regulatory policy. He describes the current federal-state tension as the "worst of both worlds."[10] The best way to solve the problem, Hudak says, is to legalize marijuana through congressional action. This will eliminate the uncertainties that result from changing presidential administrations.

## THE BESPOKE HIGH

In California, a state with legalized marijuana, a new trend is developing: the bespoke, or made-to-order, high. Rather than a generalized, all-purpose high, these marijuana formulations deliver specific types of highs using varying proportions of THC and CBD. For example, a user who had just returned from an exhausting overseas business trip bought a vape pen filled with a marijuana formulation called Sleep. Other bespoke formulations include Calm, Relief, Bliss, Arouse, and Passion. A new formulation, Focus, is meant to help the user concentrate on a task at hand.

In short, most people see marijuana legalization as inevitable. If it happens, marijuana will presumably join the ranks of alcohol and tobacco, becoming a product available to adults but strongly regulated and taxed. If research continues and the FDA sees fit, it will also become available for a variety of medical uses.

# ESSENTIAL
# FACTS

## EFFECTS ON THE BODY

- Increased heart rate, decreased balance and coordination, dizziness, dreaminess, and increased appetite

- At low doses: altered senses, changes in mood, impaired memory, and an altered sense of time

- At high doses: delusions, hallucinations, or psychosis

- Long-term effects: lung irritation, bronchitis, more frequent colds, lack of focus, and worsening of mental illnesses

- Medical uses: treatment of pain, childhood epilepsy, multiple sclerosis, and glaucoma

- Addiction: approximately 9 percent of marijuana users become addicted, with risk of addiction highest among those who start using marijuana as teens or who use the drug daily

## LAWS AND POLICIES

In 1937, the Marijuana Tax Act put marijuana under the control of the DEA. In 1970, the Controlled Substances Act classified marijuana as a Schedule I drug, indicating a high potential for abuse and no medical value. In 1996, California became the first state to create its own marijuana laws. At first, states legalized marijuana only for medical uses, but later, some began to legalize it for recreational uses as well. As of 2017, 29 states had legalized medical marijuana; another 9 states and Washington, DC, had legalized recreational marijuana. This put them in conflict with the federal government.

## IMPACT ON SOCIETY

- Marijuana is the most used illegal drug in the United States.

- Adolescents who become users can show increased problems throughout life, from not finishing high school to unemployment and decreased income. With heavy or daily doses, users can show mental health issues. But people do not die from overdoses, and addiction is relatively rare and mild.

- Because marijuana is illegal at the federal level and in many states, arrests for its possession, use, and sale are high, and sentences are often long. One result is overcrowded prisons. Another is a huge number of people who become convicted felons because they were caught with a few ounces of marijuana. Once released, they are often unable to obtain jobs, loans, housing, and other benefits.

- In states where legalization has occurred, marijuana has become a thriving business and an important part of the economy. Medical marijuana has benefited many suffering people. Those who favor federal legalization point to the likelihood of economic growth through taxation and an influx of money that can be used for social good, such as improving schools.

## QUOTE

"There needs to be some way to assess what impact [marijuana] has under controlled conditions. That is the problem . . . it's not very controlled. We need to do careful studies."

—*Dr. Harold Pinnick, professor of chemistry, Purdue University Calumet*

### ACUPUNCTURE
The practice of using needles to pierce specific parts of the body for the purpose of pain relief or disease treatment.

### ARRHYTHMIA
A condition in which the heart beats irregularly.

### CENTRAL NERVOUS SYSTEM
The brain and spinal cord, which transmit sensory and motor impulses through the body.

### CONCENTRATED
Containing a high proportion of a specific substance, with water or other diluting substances removed.

### DECRIMINALIZATION
The removal of penalties for possession of small amounts of marijuana; possession incurs a civil fine, but no jail time or criminal record.

### EPILEPSY
A nervous system disorder that causes seizures from excessive brain activity.

### EXTRACT
A concentrated form of a substance.

### LYMPHATIC SYSTEM
The body system of vessels and lymph nodes that circulates lymph—a liquid that contains white blood cells—through the body.

## MOLECULE

The smallest unit into which a substance can be broken down that is made of two or more atoms and has all of the same properties of the original substance.

## NICOTINE

A chemical compound in tobacco that acts as a stimulant.

## OPIOID

A class of drugs that act on the central nervous system to relieve pain.

## PSYCHOSIS

A period of mental and emotional impairment during which a person loses touch with reality, causing him or her to act strangely and believe things that are not true.

## RESIN

A thick, sticky substance produced by certain plants or trees.

## SCHIZOPHRENIA

A mental illness in which a person has a distorted view and understanding of the world that interferes with his or her ability to function normally; the person thinks, feels, and behaves abnormally.

## STRAIN

A group of cultivated plants with distinctive qualities.

## SYNTHETIC

Made by combining chemicals, typically to imitate a natural product.

## SELECTED BIBLIOGRAPHY

Boffey, Philip M. "What Science Says about Marijuana." *New York Times*. New York Times Company, 30 July 2014. Web. 1 Nov. 2017.

Cicero, Karen. "How Effective Is Medical Marijuana? Here's a Closer Look at 14 Different Uses." *Prevention*. Hearst Communications, 22 Apr. 2015. Web. 1 Nov. 2017.

Crawford, Alejandro. "What Have We Been Smoking?" *US News & World Report*. US News & World Report, 13 July 2015. Web. 1 Nov. 2017.

"What Is Marijuana?" *National Institute on Drug Abuse*. National Institutes of Health, Aug. 2017. Web. 1 Nov. 2017.

## FURTHER READINGS

Benjamin, Daniel. *Marijuana*. New York: Marshall Cavendish, 2014. Print.

Morgan, Kayla. *Legalizing Marijuana*. Minneapolis: Abdo, 2011. Print.

## ONLINE RESOURCES

**Booklinks**
NONFICTION NETWORK
FREE! ONLINE NONFICTION RESOURCES

To learn more about marijuana, visit **abdobooklinks.com.** These links are routinely monitored and updated to provide the most current information available.

# MORE INFORMATION

For more information on this subject, contact or visit the following organizations:

DEA MUSEUM

700 Army Navy Drive
Arlington, VA 22202
202-307-3463
deamuseum.org

Offering free admission, the DEA Museum seeks to educate the public on the history of drugs, addiction, and drug law enforcement in the United States.

NATIONAL CANNABIS INDUSTRY ASSOCIATION

126 C Street NW, Third Floor
Washington, DC 20001
888-683-5650
thecannabisindustry.org

This marijuana industry trade association publicly advocates for the emerging cannabis industry and works to develop a favorable social, economic, and legal environment for cannabis in the United States.

NATIONAL INSTITUTE ON DRUG ABUSE

Offices of Science and Policy Communications
6001 Executive Boulevard, Room 5213, MSC 9561
Rockville, MD 20852
301-443-1124
drugabuse.gov

This government agency is charged with advancing the study of drug use and addiction and applying that science to improve public health.

## CHAPTER 1. A CONTROVERSIAL DRUG

1. Carly Schwartz. "Meet the Children Who Rely on Marijuana to Survive." *Huffington Post*. Oath, 16 June 2017. Web. 15 Oct. 2017.

2. CNN Wire. "More Medical Marijuana Refugees Moving to Colorado." *Fox News 31*. Tribune Broadcasting, 10 Mar. 2014. Web. 15 Oct. 2017.

3. CNN Wire, "More Medical Marijuana Refugees Moving to Colorado."

4. CNN Wire, "More Medical Marijuana Refugees Moving to Colorado."

5. "When Weed Is the Cure: A Doctor's Case for Medical Marijuana." *Shots: Health News from NPR*. NPR, 14 July 2015. Web. 15 Oct. 2017.

6. Michael Kirsch. "This Doctor Is against Medical Marijuana. Here's Why." *KevinMD.com*. MedPage Today, 26 Sept. 2016. Web. 20 Oct. 2017.

7. Kirsch, "This Doctor Is against Medical Marijuana. Here's Why."

8. Patrick McGreevy. "Legal Marijuana Could Be a $5-Billion Boon to California's Economy." *Los Angeles Times*. Los Angeles Times, 11 June 2017. Web. 26 Jan. 2018.

9. "What Is the Scope of Marijuana Use in the United States?" *National Institute on Drug Abuse*. National Institutes of Health, Dec. 2017. Web. 10 Jan. 2018.

10. Lloyd Johnston, et al. *Monitoring the Future National Survey Results on Drug Use, 1975–2016: Overview, Key Findings on Adolescent Drug Use*. Ann Arbor, MI: Institute for Social Research, University of Michigan, 2017. Web. 25 Oct. 2017.

11. Agata Blaszczak-Boxe. "Marijuana's History: How One Plant Spread through the World." *LiveScience*. Purch, 17 Oct. 2014. Web. 25 Oct. 2017.

## CHAPTER 2. HISTORY OF MARIJUANA

1. Tia Ghose. "Marijuana: Facts about Cannabis." *Live Science*. Purch, 18 May 2017. Web. 18 Nov. 2017.

2. "History of Hemp." *Hemp.com*. Global Hemp Holdings, n.d. Web. 30 Oct. 2017.

3. "Marijuana Timeline." *PBS Frontline*. WGBH Educational Foundation, n.d. Web. 18 Nov. 2017.

4. Matt Thompson. "The Mysterious History of 'Marijuana.'" *NPR*. NPR, 22 July 2013. Web. 20 Oct. 2017.

5. Radley Balko. "Orgies, Devil Men and Knife-Wielding Maniacs: A Quick History of Cannabis Hysteria in California." *Washington Post*. Washington Post, 9 Jan. 2018. Web. 26 Jan. 2018.

6. Balko, "Orgies, Devil Men and Knife-Wielding Maniacs."

7. Thompson, "The Mysterious History of 'Marijuana.'"

8. Alejandro Crawford. "What Have We Been Smoking?" *US News & World Report*. US News & World Report, 13 July 2015. Web. 20 Oct. 2017.

9. "United States of America 1789 (rev. 1992)." *Constitution*. Constitution Project, n.d. Web. 14 Jan. 2018.

10. Joseph Misulonas. "These Charts Show the Evolution of America's Marijuana Laws over Time." *Civilized*. Civilized, 31 Aug. 2017. Web. 5 Nov. 2017.

## CHAPTER 3. MARIJUANA AND ITS EFFECTS

1. "What Is Marijuana?" *Foundation for a Drug-Free World*. Foundation for a Drug-Free World, n.d. Web. 25 Oct. 2017.

2. L. Anderson. "Marijuana: Effects, Medical Uses and Legalization." *Drugs.com*. Drugs.com, 27 Nov. 2017. Web. 1 Dec. 2017.

3. "What Is Marijuana?" *National Institute on Drug Abuse*. National Institutes of Health, Aug. 2017. Web. 25 Oct. 2017.

4. Hal Arkowitz and Scott Lilienfeld. "Experts Tell the Truth about Pot." *Scientific American*. Nature America, 1 Mar. 2012. Web. 10 Dec. 2017.

## CHAPTER 4. MEDICAL MARIJUANA

1. Shaunacy Ferro. "It's Incredibly Difficult to Study Medical Marijuana." *Business Insider*. Business Insider, 12 Aug. 2013. Web. 30 Oct. 2017.

2. Ferro, "It's Incredibly Difficult to Study Medical Marijuana."

3. "Number of Legal Medical Marijuana Patients." *ProCon*. ProCon.org, 3 Mar. 2016. Web. 11 Dec. 2017.

4. Sarah Wilson and Rachel Blevins. "Big Pharma Losing Grip as Study Shows Nearly 100% Cannabis Users Give Up Rx Pain Meds." *USA Health Note*. USA Health Note, 22 Sept. 2017. Web. 30 Oct. 2017.

5. "About Marijuana: Introduction." *NORML*. NORML and NORML Foundation, n.d. Web. 12 Nov. 2017.

6. "Average Price Per Ounce of High Quality Marijuana as of November 2017, by US State (in US Dollars)." *Statista*. Statista, Nov. 2017. Web. 11 Dec. 2017.

7. "What's the Future of Medical Marijuana?" *All Bud*. All Bud, 6 Apr. 2014. Web. 30 Oct. 2017.

8. Lesly Bailey. "Despite Legalization, Medical Marijuana's Future in Question." *NWI Times*. NWI Times, 24 Aug. 2014. Web. 30 Oct. 2017.

9. Ferro, "It's Incredibly Difficult to Study Medical Marijuana."

## CHAPTER 5. MARIJUANA VERSUS TOBACCO AND ALCOHOL

1. Paul Armentano. "Health and Societal Costs of Marijuana vs. Alcohol and Tobacco: Prohibitionists' Concerns Answered and Refuted." *Alternet*. Alternet, 30 Mar. 2012. Web. 30 Oct. 2017.

2. "No High Risk: Marijuana May Be Less Harmful Than Alcohol, Tobacco." *NBC News*. NBC News, 26 Feb. 2015. Web. 30 Oct. 2017.

3. "Smoking & Tobacco Use." *Centers for Disease Control and Prevention*. US Department of Health and Human Services, 29 Mar. 2017. Web. 30 Oct. 2017.

4. "No High Risk: Marijuana May Be Less Harmful Than Alcohol, Tobacco."

5. Rebecca Ahrnsbrak, et al. "Key Substances Use and Mental Health Indicators in the United States: Results from the 2016 National Survey on Drug Use and Health." *Substance Abuse and Mental Health Administration*. Center for Behavioral Health Statistics and Quality, 2017. Web. 11 Dec. 2017.

6. Dana Tims. "Is Marijuana Less Addictive Than Both Alcohol and Tobacco?" *PolitiFact Oregon*. Tampa Bay Times, 4 June 2014. Web. 30 Oct. 2017.

7. Olga Khazan. "Is Marijuana More Addictive Than Alcohol?" *Atlantic*. Atlantic Monthly Group, 17 Sept. 2014. Web. 1 Nov. 2017.

8. B. H. Carlini. "Marijuana and Tobacco Use." *Learn About Marijuana: Science-Based Information for the Public*. UW Alcohol & Drug Abuse Institute, Aug. 2017. Web. 1 Nov. 2017.

9. Leland Kim. "Marijuana Shown to Be Less Damaging to Lungs than Tobacco." *University of California San Francisco*. Regents of the University of California, 10 Jan. 2012. Web. 1 Nov. 2017.

10. Jennifer Welsh and Kevin Loria. "23 Health Benefits of Marijuana." *Business Insider*. Business Insider, 20 Apr. 2014. Web. 1 Nov. 2017.

11. "What Is Marijuana?" *Foundation for a Drug-Free World*. Foundation for a Drug-Free World, n.d. Web. 25 Oct. 2017.

12. "Respiratory Effects of Marijuana." *Learn About Marijuana: Science-Based Information for the Public*. UW Alcohol & Drug Abuse Institute, June 2013. Web. 1 Nov. 2017.

## CHAPTER 6. MARIJUANA IN SOCIETY

1. Alejandro Azofeifa, et al. "National Estimates of Marijuana Use and Related Indicators—National Survey on Drug Use and Health, United States, 2002–2014." *CDC*. US Department of Health and Human Services, 2 Sept. 2016. Web. 3 Nov. 2017.

2. "What Is the Scope of Marijuana Use in the United States?" *National Institute on Drug Abuse*. National Institutes of Health, Dec. 2017. Web. 10 Jan. 2018.

3. "What Is the Scope of Marijuana Use in the United States?"

4. Kathleen Miles. "Just How Much the War on Drugs Impacts Our Overcrowded Prisons, In One Chart." *Huffington Post*. Oath, 10 Mar. 2014. Web. 3 Nov. 2017.

5. Agata Blaszczak-Boxe. "Potent Pot: Marijuana Is Stronger Now Than It Was 20 Years Ago." *LiveScience*. Purch, 8 Feb. 2016. Web. 3 Nov. 2017.

6. David Trilling. "Marijuana Legalization: Research Review on Crime and Impaired Driving." *Journalist's Resource*. Harvard Kennedy School Shorenstein Center, 23 Sept. 2016. Web. 30 Oct. 2017.

7. Trilling, "Marijuana Legalization: Research Review on Crime and Impaired Driving."

8. Alejandro Crawford. "What Have We Been Smoking?" *US News & World Report*. US News & World Report, 13 July 2015. Web. 20 Oct. 2017.

9. Crawford, "What Have We Been Smoking?"

10. Christopher Ingraham. "Marijuana Arrests Fall to Lowest Level Since 1996." *Washington Post*. Washington Post, 26 Sept. 2016. Web. 11 Dec. 2017.

11. "Report: The War on Marijuana in Black and White." *ACLU*. ACLU, June 2013. Web. 3 Nov. 2017.

12. "Racial Disparity in Marijuana Arrests." *NORML*. NORML and NORML Foundation, n.d. Web. 3 Nov. 2017.

13. Martin Austermuhle. "It's 4/20, So Here's a Rundown on Marijuana Laws in the Washington Region." *WAMU*. American University, 20 Apr. 2017. Web. 11 Dec. 2017.

14. Maia Szalavitz. "Marijuana as a Gateway Drug: The Myth That Will Not Die." *Time*. Time, 29 Oct. 2010. Web. 3 Nov. 2017.

15. James Wilt. "Growing Weed Is Pretty Bad for the Environment." *Vice*. Vice Media, 18 Apr. 2017. Web. 11 Dec. 2017.

## CHAPTER 7. TO LEGALIZE OR NOT TO LEGALIZE

1. Spencer Buell. "Marijuana Is Only 'Slightly Less Awful' Than Heroin." *Boston Magazine*. Metro Corp, 15 Mar. 2017. Web. 5 Nov. 2017.

2. Buell, "Marijuana Is Only 'Slightly Less Awful' Than Heroin."

3. Jennifer De Pinto, et al. "Marijuana Legalization Support at an All-Time High." *CBS News*. CBS Interactive, 20 Apr. 2017. Web. 5 Nov. 2017.

4. Harrison Jacobs. "The DEA Treats Heroin and Marijuana as Equally Dangerous Drugs." *Business Insider*. Business Insider, 22 May 2016. Web. 7 Nov. 2017.

5. Seth Motel. "6 Facts About Marijuana." *Fact Tank*. Pew Research Center, 14 Apr. 2015. Web. 10 Dec. 2017.

6. Jimmy Carter. "Drug Abuse Message to the Congress." *American Presidency Project*. Gerhard Peters and John T. Woolley, 2 Aug. 1977. Web. 11 Dec. 2017.

7. Joseph Misulonas. "These Charts Show the Evolution of America's Marijuana Laws Over Time." *Civilized*. Civilized, 31 Aug. 2017. Web. 5 Nov. 2017.

8. "Statistics and Resources." *Colorado Department of Revenue*. State of Colorado, n.d. Web. 10 Dec. 2017.

9. "State Medical Marijuana Laws." *NCSL*. National Conference of State Legislatures, 1 Feb. 2018. Web. 6 Feb. 2018.

10. Kevin A. Sabet. "The Case against Medical Marijuana." *The Fix*. The Fix, 30 Nov. 2011. Web. 7 Nov. 2017.

11. "Marijuana Decriminalization & Its Impact on Use." *NORML*. NORML and NORML Foundation, n.d. Web. 5 Nov. 2017.

12. David Trilling. "Marijuana Legalization: Research Review on Crime and Impaired Driving." *Journalist's Resource*. Harvard Kennedy School Shorenstein Center, 23 Sept. 2016. Web. 30 Oct. 2017.

13. Christopher Ingraham. "After California Decriminalized Marijuana, Teen Arrest, Overdose and Dropout Rates Fell." *Washington Post*. Washington Post, 15 Oct. 2014. Web. 7 Nov. 2017.

14. Trilling, "Marijuana Legalization: Research Review on Crime and Impaired Driving."

15. "Does Legalizing Cannabis Reduce Crime?" *PotGuide.com*. PotGuide, 25 June 2017. Web. 7 Nov. 2017.

16. Angela Dills, Sietse Goffard, and Jeffrey Miron. "Dose of Reality: The Effect of State Marijuana Legalizations." *Policy Analysis No. 799*. Cato Institute, 16 Sept. 2016. Web. 7 Nov. 2017.

## CHAPTER 8. MARIJUANA TODAY AND TOMORROW

1. "Marijuana Laws." *Deep Dive: Marijuana*. National Conference of State Legislatures, n.d. Web. 6 Feb. 2018.

2. Harrison Jacobs. "The DEA Treats Heroin and Marijuana as Equally Dangerous Drugs." *Business Insider*. Business Insider, 22 May 2016. Web. 7 Nov. 2017.

3. Carrie Johnson. "DEA Rejects Attempt to Loosen Federal Restrictions on Marijuana." *NPR*. NPR, 10 Aug. 2016. Web. 7 Nov. 2017.

4. Alejandro Crawford. "What Have We Been Smoking?" *US News & World Report*. US News & World Report, 13 July 2015. Web. 20 Oct. 2017.

5. Josh Harkinson, Brett Brownell, and Julia Lurie. "24 Mind-Blowing Facts about Marijuana Production in America." *Mother Jones*. Foundation for National Progress, Mar./Apr. 2014. Web. 11 Dec. 2017.

6. Katie Lobosco. "The First City to Open Its Own Pot Shop." *CNN Money*. Time Warner, 10 Mar. 2015. Web. 11 Dec. 2017.

7. Katie Zezima. "Wildfires Scorched Marijuana Crops, Possibly Complicating California's Rollout of Legal Sales." *Washington Post*. Washington Post, 20 Oct. 2017. Web. 11 Dec. 2017.

8. Katie Hunt. "Report: Cheaper, Purer Illegal Substances Suggest Global War on Drugs Is Failing." *CNN*. Turner Broadcasting, 1 Oct. 2013. Web. 11 Dec. 2017.

9. Debra Borchardt. "Marijuana Sales Totaled $6.7 Billion in 2016." *Forbes*. Forbes, 3 Jan. 2017. Web. 10 Dec. 2017.

10. Phillip Smith. "This is the Future of Marijuana." *AlterNet*. AlterNet Media, 18 Jan. 2017. Web. 10 Dec. 2017.

Carol Hand has a PhD in zoology. She has taught college biology (including courses on human anatomy and physiology and on drugs), written biology assessments for national assessment companies, written middle and high school science curricula for a national company, and authored more than 40 young-adult science books, including several on health topics. Currently she works as a freelance science writer.